State of Vermont
Department of Libraries
Midstate Regional Library
RFD #4
Montpelier, Vt. 05602

WITHDRAWN

THE TIGER
THAT BARKS

BOOKS BY ALEX WHITNEY

STIFF EARS
Animal Folktales of the North American Indians

ONCE A BRIGHT RED TIGER

VOICES IN THE WIND
Central and South American Legends

SPORTS AND GAMES THE INDIANS GAVE US

PADS FOR PETS
How to Make Habitats and Other Equipment
for Small Animals

THE TIGER THAT BARKS
The True Picture
Story of Mohan and His Friends

THE TIGER THAT BARKS

The True Picture Story of Mohan
and His Friends

Alex Whitney
photos by Beverly Ecker

David McKay Company, Inc. New York

Copyright © 1978 by Alex Whitney and Beverly Ecker
All rights reserved, including the right to reproduce this book, or parts thereof, in any form, except for the inclusion of brief quotations in a review.

Library of Congress Cataloging in Publication Data

Whitney, Alex.
  The tiger that barks.

  SUMMARY: A young boy raises a Siberian tiger cub with a German shepherd.
  1. Tigers as pets—Juvenile literature. 2. Tigers—Legends and stories. 3. German shepherd dogs—Legends and stories. [1. Tigers as pets. 2. German shepherd dogs. 3. Pets] I. Ecker, Beverly. II. Title.
SF459.T46W47   636.8'9   78-5203
ISBN 0-679-20976-X

10-9-8-7-6-5-4-3-2-1
Manufactured in the United States of America

Acknowledgements

Photo, page x, courtesy of Six Flags-Great Adventure, Jackson, New Jersey.

The author and photographer wish to thank Marie and Nils Ostberg and Trudy and John Taylor for their help in the preparation of the book.

For David, Chris, Brian, Zeke, and Mohan, all of whom we greatly admire.

CONTENTS

THE SETTING 1

MOHAN'S NEW HOME 9

BRIAN AND THE ODD COUPLE 15

SPRING TRAINING 21

VANISHING SPECIES 25

MOHAN EARNS HIS STRIPES 31

GROWING UP 37

A BIG SURPRISE 41

OLD FRIENDS 47

THE SETTING

One crisp autumn day, in the pine-barren country of New Jersey, a Siberian tigress named Tanya gave birth to a litter of cubs.

Tanya is a star performer in David McMillan's wild animal show which is staged in the arena of a 1500-acre park where more than 2,000 wild animals roam freely.

David McMillan is one of the world's foremost trainers and breeders of wild animals. His magnificent big cats—twenty-one Siberian and Royal Bengal tigers, one African lion, and two Asian leopards—are featured in his show.

David has an unusual method of handling his animals. He uses no weapons and he has no backup—a person who stands by with a loaded gun in case the trainer is attacked. Instead, David relies on his own instincts and experience,

a reward system, and a great amount of patience. He must always be one step ahead of his animals. If he lost control of them for even a moment, it could be his last mistake. David carries a whip, but it's used mainly for show and for the noise it makes. The cracking sound, made by a shoelace tied to the end of the whip, distracts an animal from causing trouble.

David and his wife Chris live in a house near the park with their son Brian, and Brian's constant companion, Zeke, a German Shepherd. When Zeke was a five-month-old puppy, he became a member of the McMillan household. This was about the same time that Tanya's cubs were born.

MOHAN'S NEW HOME

When one of Tanya's babies—a tiny cub named Mohan—became ill with colic, his mother refused to nurse him. Tanya's rejection of her offspring worried David because young tigers often die of colic. Since Siberian tigers are an endangered species (fewer than seventy are left in the wild), David decided to take Mohan home, where Brian could look after him.

Brian was delighted with the new arrival. "It's like having a big, tame kitten!" he exclaimed.

"Not quite," said his father. "No one can ever truly tame a tiger. But if you handle Mohan carefully, the same way you've seen me handle the big tigers, the cub may learn to love and trust you as much as Zeke does."

Brian gingerly picked up the faintly mewing cub and held him, while Chris filled a baby's bottle with a special milk formula.

"Mohan must have a bottle every two hours," David said. "Because he has colic, he must also be burped like a baby after each feeding."

As soon as Mohan was fed and burped, David told Brian that it was time for the cub to meet Zeke.

"Dogs and cats—both wild and tame—are natural enemies," said David, "but Mohan and Zeke are babies, and they don't know this. I hope they'll get along because the companionship of another animal may keep the cub from crying for his mother all night."

When Mohan was placed in Zeke's enclosure, the puppy sniffed curiously at the furry bundle. Mohan, without once extending his sharp, inch-long claws, took a few playful swats at Zeke. Then, the little cub and the puppy played together until both grew drowsy. When at last they fell asleep, they nestled close to one another.

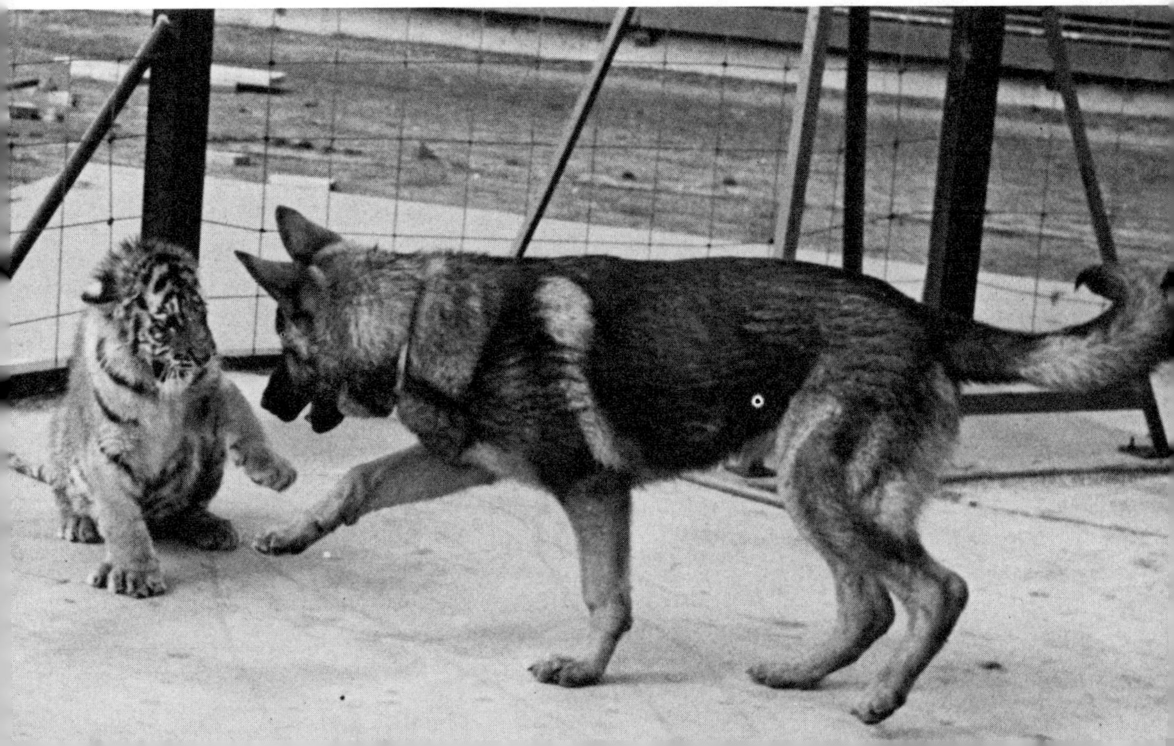

This was the beginning of a lasting friendship.

BRIAN AND THE ODD COUPLE

Mohan recovered fully from his colic within a few weeks. By that time, he and Zeke were inseparable. They roughhoused together, slept in the same enclosure, ate together, and shared the same food and water dishes.

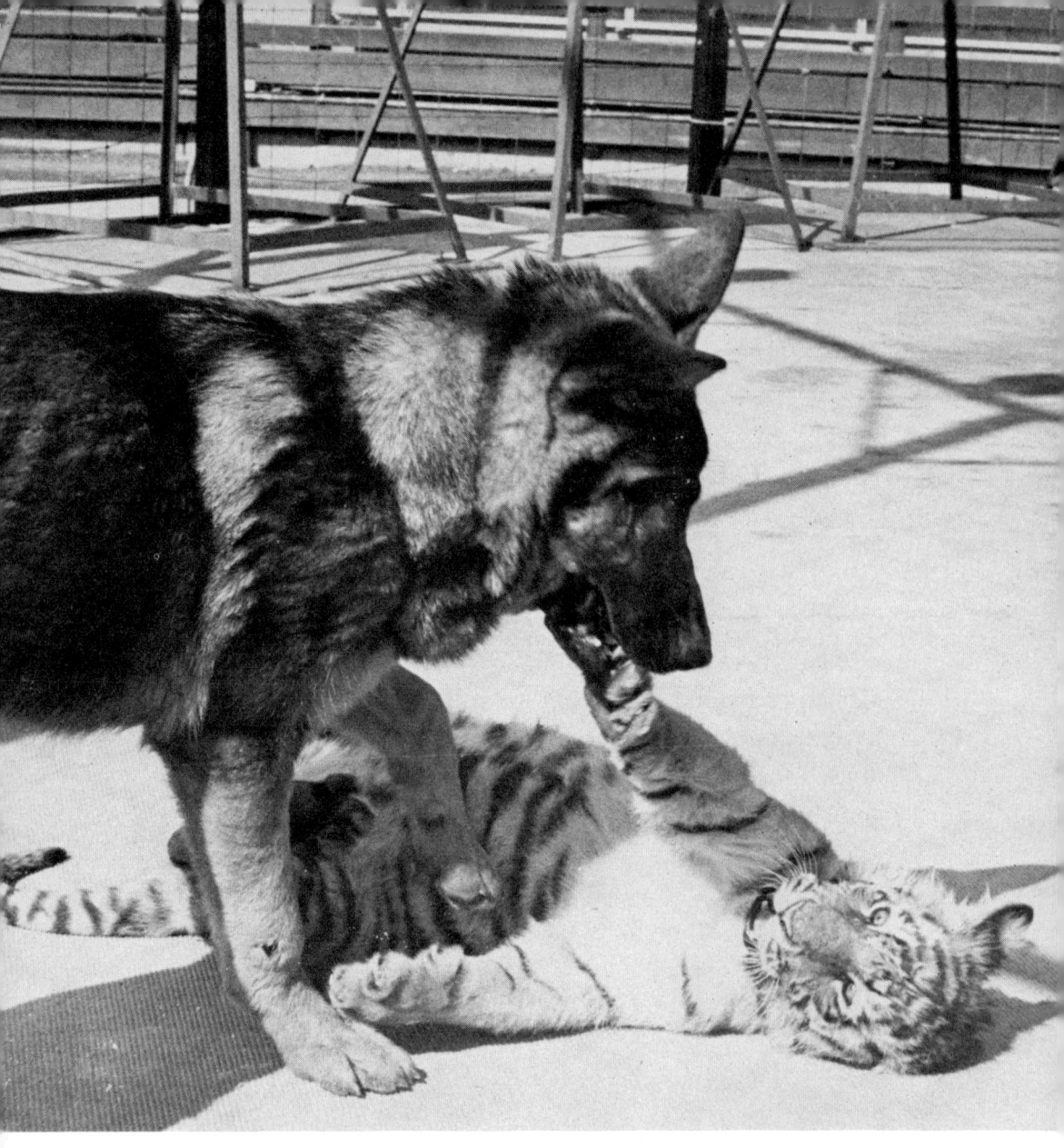

Before long, they even began to sound alike. To everyone's surprise, Mohan learned to bark!

It was clear from the start of the cub and puppy's friendship that Zeke was the boss. If Zeke grew tired of playing with Mohan, he growled or barked at the cub. Every time Zeke expressed his disfavor, Mohan rolled over on his back and closed his eyes—a tiger's way of admitting defeat.

Because the late autumn weather was unusually mild, Mohan and Zeke often romped together outdoors. Brian was their trusted playmate. They spent many hours exploring a deserted amusement park, where the workmen let them ride in the bumper cars.

The trio's favorite pastime was a game Brian called "chase," a version of hide-and-seek in which Brian ran about in search of a hiding place while Mohan followed like a shadow. The boy and the cub crouched behind bushes and huddled behind trees.

But, no matter where they hid, Zeke soon found them.

SPRING TRAINING

Mohan grew much larger during the winter months. By early spring, he was old enough to begin his basic training.

"It's a good thing Mohan still likes his bottle," David told Brian. "You can reward him with milk and small chunks of meat each time he learns a lesson."

After he taught Mohan to walk on a leash, Brian told his father that he wanted to train the cub to sit erect on his haunches, the same way the big tigers sit when they perform in the arena.

"Zeke has learned how to shake hands and sit up," Brian said. "Mohan should learn to do a trick, too."

"If you can teach Mohan to sit erect, you and the cub and Zeke can present your own act in one of my shows," David said. "We'll bill you as *Brian McMillan and His Fabulous Dog and Tiger.*"

Brian McMillan and His Fabulous Dog and Tiger. Brian smiled blissfully as he repeated the words to himself.

He began Mohan's training program that day. First, Brian placed Mohan on a small pedestal and encouraged Zeke to sit on a stool beside the cub. Then, he told Zeke to sit up, and the dog promptly did so. But, when Brian urged Mohan to do likewise, the cub bared his teeth, snarled, barked, and laid down.

Brian tirelessly repeated the commands, but, more often than not, Mohan refused to obey them. Only the sight of rewards—pieces of meat and a bottle of milk—could revive the cub's interest in the training procedure.

"Tigers learn by repetition. The same behavior must be practiced over and over again," David told Brian that evening. "You must be stricter with the cub, and you must never reward him until he has done what you want him to do. If you give Mohan too much food, he'll become lazy and he'll want to do what you and I want to do after a full meal—sleep."

VANISHING SPECIES

During the early part of the summer, Brian spent most of each day training Mohan or playing with him. But the cub was left at home when Brian and Zeke accompanied David on his daily rounds.

Brian carried trays of food and pails of water to his father's tigers and the other animals, all of which are endangered species.

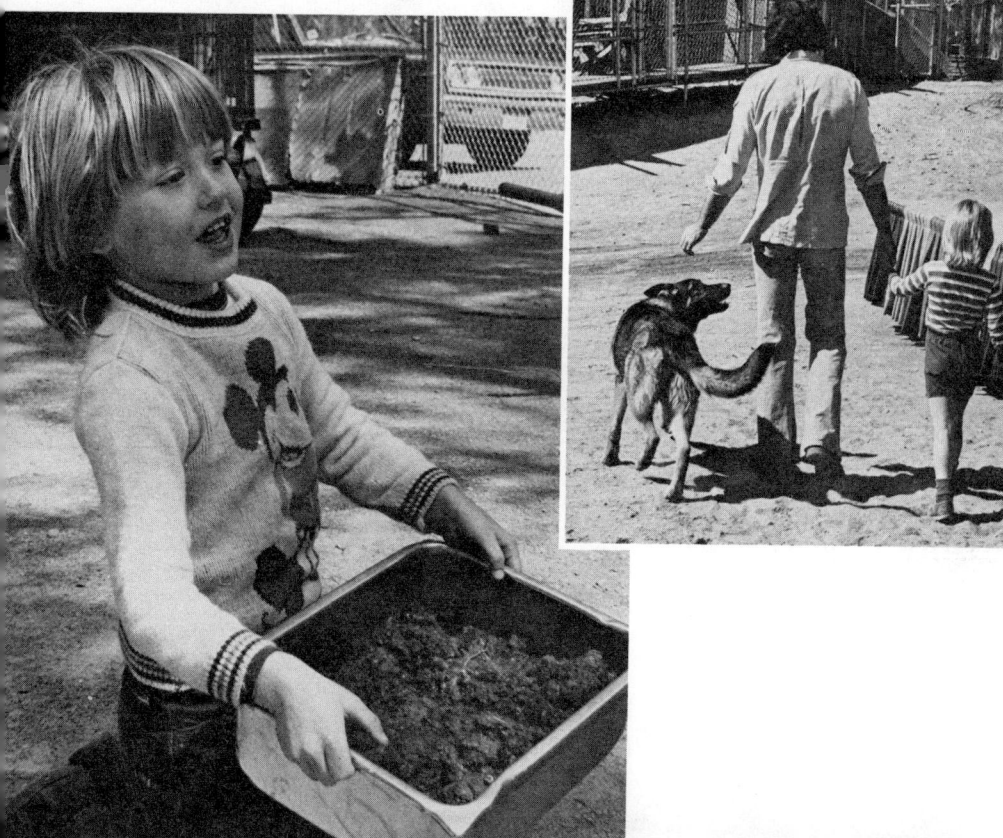

They included Pancho, the African lion . . .

Angel, the spotted Asian leopard . . .
Nina, the panther (actually a black leopard) . . .

Carla, the North American black bear Chris trained to dance, wave, kiss, and play basketball ...

and Max, the timber wolf.

None of the species were declawed or defanged. Each had clean, well-kept quarters and roomy exercise areas. Brian knew the animals would lead content and healthy lives in captivity.

David explained why this was so: "Providing they're well cared for, wild animals live longer and even breed in captivity. If they're sick or injured, they can be treated by veterinarians. In the wild, animals are at the mercy of their predators—including people. They're also victims of their own beauty. Tigers, for instance, are still being illegally hunted and killed in Asia because a single tiger skin is worth thousands of dollars. And many years ago, professional bounty hunters killed countless numbers of bears, timber wolves, and other wild animals that once flourished in North America."

MOHAN EARNS HIS STRIPES

Brian was awake long before sunrise on the day he, Zeke, and Mohan were scheduled to perform in David's show.

After Brian gave Zeke a bath and brushed Mohan's coat until it shone, he put on his new costume.

As the threesome sat by the entrance to the arena waiting for their cue to enter the ring, Brian had a sudden pang of doubt.

"You won't forget what I've taught you to do, will you, Mohan?" he asked the cub. Mohan licked Brian's face, as if to reassure him.

Brian listened to the familiar sounds of his father's show: the snarls and low rumbles of the tigers as they leaped on their assigned pedestals and formed a pyramid; the sharp crack of David's whip just before Tanya sprang from a high perch and soared through a hoop of fire.

Over the blare of piped-in music, Brian heard his father's voice, "I would like to introduce three new performers—Brian McMillan and his fabulous dog and tiger."

Brian went into the ring. He squinted his eyes against the bright sunlight and saw Mohan's green and gold eyes peering back at him. The cub and Zeke had taken their places on two low stools.

From then on everything went as smoothly as Brian had hoped it would. When he gave the command, Zeke sat up and begged and Mohan sat erect on his haunches and waved his forepaws in the air. The audience clapped and cheered.

Brian's face was flushed with heat and pride as he and his father took their bows.

"Now everyone will know I'm Brian the Animal Trainer!" he told his father.

GROWING UP

Toward the end of summer, David knew that Mohan and Brian would soon have to be separated. The cub's soft baby fur had been replaced by a thick, tawny gold-and-black coat, and he outweighed Brian by more than 100 pounds.

When David told Brian that Mohan would have to leave, Brian pleaded with his father, "Can't I please keep him, Dad? Mohan loves me!"

"It would be too risky," David replied. "Tigers are fierce predators, and they always retain their natural instincts. Some may be very affectionate, but they may turn on a person without warning. Even if Mohan continued to be as friendly as he is now, he might accidently injure you while he's playing. In another month, he'll be much larger and heavier. If he isn't disciplined and trained with the big tigers now, he'll be impossible to control later on."

The thought of life without Mohan made Brian miserable. But he gradually began to realize the truth in what his father had told him. When the boy took Mohan for his daily walks, the cub often refused to go in the direction he was being led. Somehow Mohan sensed that his weight and strength could be used to his own advantage. Although Brian kept a firm grasp on Mohan's leash, no amount of coaxing or pulling had any affect if the tiger stubbornly refused to budge.

When the time came for Mohan to move to his new quarters with the other tigers, Brian flung his arms around the cub. "I'll never forget you, Mohan," he cried. "You'll always be *my* tiger!"

Brian brushed the tears from his eyes and clung to Zeke as David led Mohan away.

A BIG SURPRISE

One morning, shortly after Mohan's departure, David told Brian that he had a big surprise for him.

"A bigger surprise than Mohan?" Brian asked.

"Much bigger," said David. "How would you like to have another pet, one that's fully grown and will probably live until she's seventy years old? I won't tell you what the animal is, but perhaps you'll guess."

Brian was filled with curiosity as he followed his father to the pick-up truck and climbed into the front seat. David drove the truck along a winding road, through an open gate, and up the slope of a wooded hill.

Brian saw an animal that left him breathless. Never before had he felt so small.

"This is Gypsy," David said. "She's an Indian elephant, and she was born in the wild twenty-five years ago. Her former owner taught her to do several tricks, and you and I will train her to do more."

"Wow!" said Brian. "What do we feed her?"

"Three bales of hay, ten pounds of fruit, five pounds of bran, and about forty gallons of water daily," said David. "Elephants are the largest land mammals in the world, and they eat and drink constantly for eighteen hours each day. You can take Gypsy for walks and let her scratch her hide on the trunks of trees. And you can ride on her."

"Someday I'll have a great act," Brian said. "Brian McMillan Presents His Fabulous Dog and Tiger *and* His Surprising Elephant!"

OLD FRIENDS

Although Brian and Zeke spent much of their time with Gypsy, they visited Mohan every day until the park closed for the season. Brian was not allowed to be alone with the cub unless David was present, but Zeke still played with Mohan in the tiger's enclosure. And, strangely enough, Zeke was still the boss, even though Mohan was more than twice the dog's size.

Brian and Zeke often sat in the audience and watched Mohan when he was in the ring with the other tigers. In addition to sitting erect, the cub could also roll over. But Brian knew that Mohan would need a full season of training before he learned how to perform in David's show.

Mohan's place in the ring had been carefully chosen. On each side of the cub's pedestal were two tigers who were friendly to him. He was usually chained to the wire fence because, if Mohan left his pedestal, he might have been attacked by another tiger.

How did Mohan react to his new lifestyle? Most of the time he sat on his perch, now and then uttering a sound that Brian described as a "barrowl," a combination of a bark and a growl.

Whenever David wasn't looking, Mohan turned and poked his nose through the wire. Then, he gazed intently at the crowd as if he hoped to catch sight of a small boy and a German shepherd.

j636.89
Whitney, A
 The tiger that barks

MRL

WITHDRAWN
NOV 14 1983

State of Vermont
Department of Libraries
Midstate Regional Library
RFD #4
Montpelier, Vt. 05602

Date Due

FEB. 2 1988

MAR. 25 1988

VERMONT DEPT. OF LIBRARIES
0 0001 0281941 4

Printed in U.S.A.